To Helen
for Heavenly timing

Charlie Shedd

"Whenever we feel put upon with details, frantic with schedules, wearied by demands, it is probable that we have been listening to the world and not to the Lord. Men will give us excessive burdens. Our earthly directors will prescribe too much for us. But we have this sacred promise, 'He will never let you be tempted, beyond what you can stand.' (I Cor. 10:13 Moffatt) We discover our peace when we discover the divine pace which heaven has set for us."

"Make the best possible use of your time."
—Col. 4:5 Phillips

TIME FOR ALL THINGS

Charlie W. Shedd

How a Christian Manages Time

Abingdon
NASHVILLE

TIME FOR ALL THINGS

A Festival Book

Copyright © 1962 by Abingdon Press

Festival edition published February 1980

Second printing August 1980

ISBN 0-687-42106-3

PRINTED IN THE UNITED STATES OF AMERICA

DEDICATION

To Martha who, like her namesake of the Gospels, is queen of the household arts; and who, like the sister of the same story, has the radiance of spirit which comes from dwelling long at the Master's feet.

Preface

Six years ago we moved to a new church. The people we left were great folks. They were enthusiastic supporters, hard workers, and well organized. They had just completed a majestic new building which stands as a fitting tribute to their zeal.

Our new work was with one of the thousands of embryonic churches rising out of America's suburbs. It was to be located at a strategic corner in a booming development. Our city is one of the fastest-growing urban centers of the world. We had a handful of brave souls, an old farmhouse in a wooded pasture for headquarters, a rented schoolhouse for services.

In my previous charge, when I wanted something done, I pushed a button and my selection of five staff members would come running.

Here I didn't even have a button!

Whatever I wanted these days was mine to do. There were meetings to schedule, phones to answer, stencils to cut, wastebaskets to empty, leaders

7

to recruit, fences to mend, procedures to print, teachers to get, letters to write. There were myriad matters I had taken for granted when somebody else was "working the salt mines."

In addition to these routine items there were people. First, dozens of people. Then hundreds. Then thousands. Whenever we opened the schoolhouse door it seemed that children came out of the woodwork. Children have parents and parents have friends. Before we knew it, our membership reached fifteen hundred, with twice that many on our prospect list. This was through no genius of mine. It can be credited in part to some unique programs worked into the fabric of our church by its charter leaders. But we are also frank to admit that it is partially due to circumstances which have been labeled "fate," "destiny," or "the plan of God." By whatever name, people poured in.

People take time. They get sick. They have troubles. They need to talk. People get married. They have babies. They build new homes. They want their pastor's prayers. They want him to pray for their family, their journey, their promotion. They like to share their joys with their minister. They bring their visitors to meet him. They join the church. They want something to do. They want help to do it right. They lose interest. They get their feelings hurt. They quit. They hope to be missed.

I love people. I love challenge. I love church work.

But I am also a parent. I am the father of four strong sons and one beautiful daughter. I love to be with them. They love to be with me.

But most of all I love my wife. I need to be with her more than I need any earthly thing. I operate best when I can spend great blocks of time with her. She says it's like that with her. I have complete faith in what she says.

It soon became evident in this new church that I must make some adjustments. An honest look at myself revealed that I was sick with perfectionism. I had been trained to believe that all the world was watching every little move I made. I had been raised on "What will people think?" My desk *had* to be cleared of everything, not just by nightfall, but in the next ten minutes. Letters must be answered the same day received.

There were two solutions. The first was to pass on as much work as I could to members of the church. I studied everything available on lay-participation. I am now an expert in getting someone else to do the work.

The second solution was to search seriously for inner quiet, a new serenity, a deep leisure of soul, which I had never known before.

I am still working at this. I do not have all the answers. But I am sure I have found where the answers are. I am a long way from what I ought to be. But I know One who has arrived. As I put my ear down to the Gospels I made a new discovery. The "Son of man" was life's master-manager in human form. Here was efficiency at the apex. He said he could show me how to live. He said he could guarantee results.

This was worth serious study.

CHARLIE W. SHEDD

Contents

Affirmation I

I Have Only One Thing to Do

Life's Single Holy Assignment

"Thou art careful and troubled about many things; but one thing is needful."

—LUKE 10:41-42

OUR TEEN-AGE DAUGHTER WON A science prize last winter. Her ingenious project consisted of an electronic brain with wires, bulbs, sockets, and switches. There were many other intricacies, all put together on a giant frame. Over the frame she stretched a king-size drawing of a man's head. When the lips opened to speak, lights went on and off, tracing a single word through the human skull.

No small part of the glory, however, was really due to Ben. Fortunately for us this veritable wizard is our neighbor. He can fix stoves, radios, television sets, record players, irons, sweepers, cars—almost anything.

Our junior brain builder would work diligently until some development became complex beyond her ability. Then she would carry that part to Ben's house. He would go over the work done, correct mistakes, and carefully explain how this piece fit into the master construction.

One evening Karen came home excited with the announcement: "Ben says I should bring the whole business over to his house. Instead of me taking him the parts, he wants the whole deal. Then he'll give me the parts in their right order. He says that way everything will be O.K. Isn't that neat? He's sure we'll beat the deadline now."

This homely bit of doing between a lively American schoolgirl and her engineer neighbor offers us a parable for life's right order. The holy key to proper management only comes when we give our Lord "the whole deal" and work with the parts as he gives them to us.

This is the Christian secret to great living. We are here on holy assignment. Life's true effectiveness does not result from getting God to help us. Our lives assume their maximum worth when we turn our wills over to him and ask that we might be of assistance to his purposes.

We Belong to God

Christian theology holds that "We are his workmanship, created in Christ Jesus for good works."

14

(Eph. 2:10 R.S.V.) This for us is a holy fact. Life does not belong to us. We are not "independents," free to have our own way if we can get it. We are, rather, part of a divine architectural masterpiece in which each unit has meaning in the master design.

Our astronauts gave us a good example when they disclaimed credit for America's mighty feats of space accomplishment. In true humility they contended that all this fuss should not be made over them. Instead, they pointed out that they were only the extension of years of research, months of planning, and much greater doings than one man in flight.

If we are truly God's, what counts for us is not what we are able to accomplish but what he is able to do through us. When we are at our best, we will seek only to be extensions of *his* greatness.

Naturally this does not give us license to sit carelessly by while we leave it all to God. Some things require that we be up and doing. Someone needs to tend the culinary arts when folks must be fed. Simply sitting is not prescribed when movement is a holy must. For the concerned disciple with heavenly connections, outer action and inner communion are not separate things. On the surface we may be meeting some demand which is essential, but our effectiveness will be controlled by hidden forces.

Psychologists have shown us that most normal human beings do live on two levels at once. As the housewife does her dishes she is likely to be planning her next meal. While the businessman drives his car to the office, he may be formulating important directives. The examples are all about us. This is especially true for sons and daughters of the Lord. When God is at work in us he will be breathing into our surface activities his spirit from the center. This divine communion at the core is the Christian's master secret to master management. It is the purpose for which we were born.

The Christ-directed soul will get more done because it moves away from "troubling about many things." Worldly wobble is eliminated. This life is co-ordinated. God is at work here, and God is order. When this relationship becomes reality, it quiets the inner confusion and flows in the direction of God's original intent.

Center Down in Christ

God has not left us to guess how we can best project his plans and purposes in our little lives.

The greatest implementing concept of our Christian faith is the doctrine of the Resurrection. This concept holds that Christ is a living presence who longs to live in and bring God's plan to completion in a human heart. For the true disciple of Christ, then, the art of living is the art of intimate Christly concourse deep within the secret places of the soul. If this is true, one thing stands for the Christian as life's absolute essential. *This is the Christ focusing of the soul!*

In the gospel accounts of Jesus' activities there are some intimate touches of his life with special friends. One of these, which offers an interesting illustration of life's proper order, is the story of Mary and Martha.

Jesus has come to this home for a rest, or for some other reason, but certainly for a meal. As Martha prepares the food, Mary sits at Jesus' feet intently taking in his every word. Finally, Martha, bothered by the lack of assistance, solicits the Master's support in activating her sitting sister. To which Jesus replies, "Martha, Martha, thou art careful and troubled about many things: but one thing is needful; and Mary hath chosen that good part, which shall not be taken away from her." (Luke 10:41-42.)

Although there are several ways to interpret

this story, we can improve our efficiency when we grasp what Jesus was trying to teach the two sisters and us. Martha wanted to be at her best for this meal. Jesus had been away for some time and this was an important homecoming. This dinner must be done to a queen's taste. "Drop in for potluck anytime" was not the mood of this occasion. Most of us have little sympathy for Mary's sitting. It looks to us like idle shirking. But if there is time to do only one thing, then the "one thing . . . needful" is the thing to do. And when there are countless items on our agenda, we do well to "center down in Christ" as the first business of the day.

The Christian life is the very reverse of spreading ourselves wide and thin. There will be time for all things, and all our living will be timely when our souls are inwardly concentrated on the Inner Presence. This is true Christian simplicity, and we move onto the soul's highway when we tell Christ that first of all we want to know him and let him live in us.

This is not some mystical abstraction reserved for visionaries and impractical saints. It is life's highest goal for ordinary servants of the Lord. This is the stuff of everyday assignment for modest men and women. It is holy stuff for the office and

18

kitchen, for the schoolroom and yard, for the shop and the plow. All life for the Christian is for singling the eye to Kingdom service. Such living is never easy, but God has not left us to do this alone.

The Work of the Holy Spirit

According to one of the jokes from Maine, a certain farmer was shingling his barn in the fog. The tale goes that on this particular day the fog was so thick that he shingled six feet out into the fog before he discovered he was no longer on the barn. The subject of the Holy Spirit may tend to leave us in the fog. Yet this is not unique with us.

When Paul asked certain disciples at Ephesus if they had received the Holy Spirit, they said they not only had never received him, they had never even known there was one. (Acts 19:1-2.) For some of us even today the words "Holy Spirit" are likely to be far out in the realm of the vague and mysterious. But this we know from Scripture—he comes to make Christ personal whenever we invite him. And these same scriptures describe these marvelous things he will do for us.

He will direct our conversation. When we let him speak through us he will use our lips to his glory. All three of the Gospels record Jesus' advice to his disciples that they need not be nervous in tense moments because the Holy Spirit would tell them what to say. (See Luke 12:12, Mark 13:11, Matt. 10:20.)

He is our teacher. Jesus told his followers that this Spirit will "teach you all things, and bring to your remembrance all that I have said to you" (John 14:26 R.S.V.).

He separates the genuine from the false. John 16:13 (R.S.V.) promises, "He will guide you into all the truth."

He will show us how to pray. Rom. 8:26-27 tells us that when our feeble hearts are not able to pray in the right way he searches our souls and makes prayers in agreement with the mind of God.

But in order to receive him, we must understand this: he only works his way! This is no timid guest who takes life as he finds it in our souls. He does not adapt himself quickly to things he wishes were different. He doesn't go at all for private little transactions in the soul's back chambers. He allows no small print and no provisos in the contract. He does not teach us for our own ends. He doesn't show us how to pray so that we can have what we want. Jesus said of the Holy Spirit that when he is come "he will glorify me" (John 16:14 R.S.V.).

This is how the Holy Spirit is received. Whenever we open our inmost chambers and pray, "Lord, come into my heart! Make alive your life in me. I want your way more than my way. Use my every cell and my every moment for your glory"—when we say that, and mean it, his inner presence fills our souls, and we will know him in all his radiance. We will also know that this is the "one thing . . . needful" for this day, and the days before us, and all eternity.

A Midwest banker taught me something useful about hunting ducks. He was an expert marksman who used the blind across the river from mine. One day in mid-season, he stopped me on the street with this candid observation: "You've been spoiling lots of shots for yourself and all the rest of us. Let me give you a tip. I improved my own bag 100 per cent when I quit shooting at ducks in general and learned to aim at one duck. You're probably firing at the whole flight. Try leveling down on a single bird and see what happens."

The next time out, I did what the man said, and found he was right. I had been firing wildly in the hope of hitting something. But when I focused on a single duck and stayed with it, my percentage improved as he said it would.

21

I am very grateful for this tip from my honest friend. It not only made a difference between an empty bag and some real results, but the same technique applies in other areas. Nowhere is this more true than in personal spiritual development. We have discovered life's deepest truth for the Christian when we focus our lives on Christ and let all other items come second to that.

Affirmation II

I Have as Much Time as Anyone

All the Time in the World

> *"My God shall supply all your need
> according to his riches in glory by
> Christ Jesus."*
>
> —PHIL. 4:19

JOE G. MISSED ANOTHER OPPORTUNity for promotion recently. For the third time in eleven years someone was brought in from another department to head the office where Joe had "given his all."

This time, Joe was loud in his condemnation of the company. Most of us who knew him heard his story several times. Of course, we felt for him, but in such problems there isn't much one can do, except listen.

In this case, however, I happen to have some acquaintance with those in the upper echelons of the company involved. Shortly after the big disappointment I found myself in a luncheon group where various personalities became the natural subject of conversation. I listened with real interest when the topic turned to Joe, and one of his superiors made this scathing observation:

"The guy is a latherer. You know what I mean? We had a horse like that on the farm. He'd come in at night all steamed up until you'd think he'd plowed the whole field by himself. But he didn't. He spent most of his energy blowing and puffing. We called him Ol' Bustle-Fuss! My mother named him, and sometimes she'd use the name on us. When we'd get worked up, she'd say, 'Slow down, Ol' Bustle-Fuss.'

"You'd think, to hear Joe tell it, that he had twice as much work as anyone and half as much time to get it done. No time for coffee—too busy! No time for a good laugh—too busy! So we load him up with little stuff; keep him busy with junk. We can't take a chance on him with things that count. Sure it's too bad, but what else can you do with a latherer?"

It goes without elaboration that the gentleman might not win the cup for kindness, but his sharp portrayal lacks little else.

Few things are more boring than the recitals of the overworked. These harassed and harried wailers seem to insinuate that fate has given them so much more to accomplish and so much less time to get it done.

Almost everyone feels on occasion, "I don't know where my days have gone. If only I had more time." Yet the truth is that every human soul has all the time in the world.

The Fairness of God

The impartiality of our Creator is nowhere more evident than at this point. Out of his goodness the heavenly Father has ordained that each son of Adam and every daughter of Eve daily has the same ration of hours and minutes. Such an argument breaks down as we compare the years men are given on earth. But this too levels out when we believe that we are eternal for his purposes.

Our Christian faith teaches that God has a plan for our affairs. We also hold that he is loving and wise. If then we believe that he has something in mind for us, loves us, and knows what is best for us, this must follow—he is not likely to give us an overload. Whenever we feel put upon with details, frantic with schedules, wearied by demands, it is probable that we have been listening to the world and not to the Lord. Men will give us excessive burdens. Our earthly directors will prescribe too much for us. But we have his sacred promise, "He will never let you be tempted, beyond what you can stand." (I Cor. 10:13 Moffatt.) We find our peace when we discover the divine pace which heaven has set for us.

Contentment and Satisfaction

Phil. 4:19 is one of the great promises of Holy Writ. "My God shall supply *all* your need according to his riches in glory by Christ Jesus" is all-inclusive.

This verse is usually applied to material matters. But it goes as well for our time and energy. Yet the promise says nothing about our wants. Most of us learn sooner or later that our desires and our necessities are not always equivalent. *The secret is to bring all our yearnings before the Lord for his refining.* We are to want what he wants from us. We are to understand that we were created for his purposes. When we know this truth, and live by it, we can count on him to provide the time necessary to serve his ends. To live in this knowledge is to enter a secret place of true Christian contentment.

We do well to observe that the promise of Phil. 4:19 is accompanied by the apostle's earlier word, "I have learned, in whatsoever state I am, therewith to be content" (Phil. 4:11).

There is a fine distinction worth noting here. It is possible to be content even when we are not satisfied. Satisfaction may be a long time coming. We can define satisfaction as that quality of soul which arrives when we feel we have achieved God's ultimate will. For some of us this may take considerable doing. Satisfaction is often a long-range matter.

But contentment is an ever-present feeling in the heart which comes from Christ's presence in us. As a scientist told me one day in his laboratory: "This experiment will take months and we won't be satisfied until we know our assumptions are authentic. But right now there's only one thing to do. Five times a day we check to be sure our catalyst is working and if it is we rest it there."

Contentment is the catalyst to satisfaction. It comes from the Inner Presence working out God's will in our lives. In this companionship it is possible to work at peace even when we must work hard to achieve the Lord's doing with our talents and our time.

Joe G. and all his ilk—and the same lathering waster in us—can only come to true serenity when Creator and created have become one-willed. When our souls have been harmonized with heaven there will be a fading away of those wailing voices

27

which complain that the hours are too short. Now we need no longer wave our arms in despair, nor look at our watches in frenzy, nor wipe our brows in the fevered fear that we will not get done what we are supposed to do. When Christ directs our doing, we will know that he holds us by his guiding hand, and in this knowledge is our true contentment.

This is the contentment which has learned how to wait. There is a vast difference between waiting in idleness and waiting on the Lord. Spiritual waiting is expectant waiting. It is dynamic. It does not paralyze God's plan by fretting. It does not scold. Instead it uses these moments for building up faith in the Lord of the harvest. When Christ is living in us, we refuse to hurry the budding flower. If we want results in ten days we can plant radishes. But roses take care and time and patient waiting. Great is our contentment when we learn to let go our own hold and to lay our hand on the heavenly pulse beat. This recognition that "our times are in his hands" is another of "his riches in glory by Christ Jesus."

"By Christ Jesus"

"My God shall supply all your need according to his riches in glory by Christ Jesus." These last three words of Phil. 4:19 are no mere afterthought to the promise of God's supply.

There is an attractive philosophy which appears often in the writings of the mystics. It is phrased in such terms as, "I am where I should be"—"I have been brought to this place at this moment for this work"—"No matter where I find myself, there is where I belong." This appealing thought is correct, however, only on one condition. The truth of it depends on this: Has our Lord brought us to this situation in order that he might use us, right here, right now?

For most of us the answer will require continual checking. There is a quasi contentment which may be nothing more than fatalistic resignation. We may be covering lots of ground in overdrive when God needs us pushing a load in low gear. Or perhaps we should be shifting to reverse that we might back up to where he is.

"By Christ Jesus" is life's purest contentment. By him our real needs are met. By him our wants are controlled. By his inner direction we have the wisdom to choose our use of time from countless choices good and bad. He is the holy center of reference who judges our work, directs our service, brings each new day to us, and us to each new day for what needs to be done for him.

29

His inner presence is our one thing needful. It is his one thing needful from us. In this communion we are at rest, but we are alert. We are concerned, but we are content. Christ, at his own good pace, can fit us where he needs us when he needs us for his activity. All time is ours when we are all his for the Father's plan.

Affirmation III

I Will Set Aside Moments to Be Alone with My Lord

Time to Be Quiet

"He went up into the mountain apart to pray: and when evening was come, he was there alone."

—MATT. 14:23

THE LITTLE GIRL WHO PRAYED, "Forgive us this day our daily bread," touched on a subtle possibility in her mistaken wording. There is a tendency in most of us to major in material matters while we minor in things of the spirit. Little by little each day has a way of erecting a wall between ourselves and the Lord.

Yet our all-wise heavenly Father does not free most of us from things of the earth. Other people and necessities of the body seem destined to consume great blocks of our time. Actually, these things need not be evil in themselves. But unless we set up guards they can become so. We may find ourselves involved in rendering unto Caesar the things that are Caesar's 100 per cent of our time.

Always these material needs, both present and future, can create avenues away from, or avenues toward, the Lord of life. Which way the roads point is up to us.

We have seen that the direction of these paths of dedication is everyday business for the Christian. Each simple event, and every so-called unimportant moment, may be another channel for closer divine fellowship. But commitment of this high kind will call for periods of hushed stillness while we listen to the voice of God. It will require that we use some of our time for "study to be quiet" (I Thess. 4:11).

The Master's Moments Apart

Every student of the life of Christ knows that the Master himself lived by this rule. In addition to the words, "When the evening was come, he was there alone," Matthew elsewhere shows Jesus departing "by ship into a desert place apart" (Matt. 14:13). Luke, the detail specialist of the gospel writers, in his account of the Lord's prayer says that the disciples made their famous request, "Teach us to pray," as they observed him "praying in a certain place" (Luke 11:1). It is not always clear when the Synoptic authors are telling of new events or describing again what the others have recorded. But additional passages, such as "And it came to pass, as he was alone praying" (Luke 9:18), clearly indicate that Jesus counted it time well spent sometimes to be alone in holy stillness.

The spiritual masters of every century join the witness. Their lives, too, indicate that it is more likely we will honor God at specific moments if we have aligned our lives with him in general. A daily quiet time for the Christian is toward this end.

We are not here considering certain moments when we teach a class of children on the sabbath day. This is not the hour of worship when we bow in reverence with other believers in the house of God. This regular "quiet time" is rather a precious period of personal communion. Here our days are set down in the secret center to which they belong.

In the crowded schedules of most lives such an art will require real doing. But the fact stands that most of us get done what we most want to do. In addition, God has promised to assist us when we bend our wants in his direction. The psalmist, a master at devotion himself, confirms this truth with his words, "Delight thyself also in the Lord; and he shall give thee the desires of thine heart. Commit thy way unto the Lord; trust also in him; and he shall bring it to pass." (Ps. 37:4-5.) This covenant still holds. No one who has turned all of his time over to God has ever been shortchanged in time for the life of real devotion.

Techniques for the Quiet Time

Sometimes these moments open up most naturally in the evening. For some, they may seem more fruitful in the early hours before other lives make traffic in the mind. They may come at unexpected places in the day's activity. But the important thing is to want them—to want them regularly—and to let God know that we will be ready whenever he brings us to these havens of quiet along the routes of our daily lives. The vital question is not, "What will we do in the quiet time?" It isn't, "When will we keep the quiet time?" What matters most is, "Do we really want the quiet time?"

Bob H. is a rising young executive in one of America's major oil companies. He is also a concerned Christian. Because he lives prayerfully there is real help for some of us in his witness:

"Every day, when I return from lunch," he says, "I lock my door for what I call my 'time way out.' My secretary holds off visitors, takes my phone, and never bats an eye when she says, 'He's in consultation. May I have him call?'

"What do I do? Sometimes you wouldn't think that I was doing anything. I just sit still, and thank God, and get real quiet. Or maybe I look over my schedule and imagine that God is looking at it with me. Sometimes I get down on my knees and pray. Other days I read a bit and wait till the words sink way down. Sometimes all this takes only a few minutes. But I always try to take enough time to be sure of one thing—am I a little bit more like God wants me to be?"

He describes it well. Each quiet time is different from the one before. Sometimes these periods are given to prayer itself. On other occasions it is well for us to study the masters of spiritual living. Perhaps the periods of stillness are best approached with pencil in hand as the Inner Presence gives up fresh thoughts for the waiting mind. Self-searching and confession may be the order for today, for sins, both known and unknown, will stand out in bold relief when the heart is sincere. A study of the Bible itself serves as an excellent tool for reshaping the soul.

Another telling practice for our quiet time is serious concentration on the life of Jesus. There

are many excellent books on the life of Christ in
the book markets. Maybe a red-letter edition of
the New Testament with Jesus' words set out in
color would give us what we need. The Christian
believes that no life was ever lived in such complete perfection. For the true disciple this was
the most thorough job of right living ever seen
among the sons of men.

Timewise we study his days on earth and are
overcome with awe. Given no more than three years
of actual recorded ministry, he split history in two
sections—"before" and "after" his own time. In
this brief span, he gathered to himself a motley
group and fashioned a force for building a world
kingdom. He preached sermons, taught lessons, said
things which have become the theme for several
thousand books. He established a church, wrought
a world kingdom, had time for "even the least,"
and kept great blocks of time for nothing but pure
communion with the Father. We do well to relive
his life as nearly as we can and repeatedly ask ourselves, "What would he do with these minutes and
hours if he were living in me today?"

The Greatest Fact About Prayer

It was a sharp young lady at the Youth Prayer
Group who broke the silence one morning with

her exciting discovery. The group was meditating on Rev. 3:20 when she startled the others with her words: "I get it! Prayer isn't my asking God. It's his asking me. What it means is, I don't need to beat on his door. He's already knocking on mine."

The verse which brought her to this realization may be the most perfect scriptural definition of perfect prayer: "Behold, I stand at the door, and knock: if any man hear my voice, and open the door, I will come in."

Grand new vistas come to the student of spiritual living when he understands that prayer's first act is not on the human side. The initial move of real prayer is from God. Banging at the gates of heaven in frantic appeal is prayer, of a sort. But prayer of the finer sort is hearing the knock of him who is nearer to us than breathing—closer than hands and feet.

This is the spirit of the quiet time. It is for pondering the love of God who sent his Son to die for us, to break the bonds of death for us, and to be a living presence in the hearts of those who have heard his knock. Great prayer is often much more simple than we are prone to think. When we tend to worry about phrasing, we might do well sometimes to reduce all wording to the plain two words, "Come in!"

This is the reason for our daily devotions. Things mighty and minor, things many and much; things of the everyday—whether these things are full of sound and fury or all serene depends on this: Do they stem from an inner center where God's holy oneness is being fashioned in our hearts?

Affirmation IV

I Will Welcome My Lord to My Subconscious

Clearing the Back Room

"If any man be in Christ, he is a new creature: old things are passed away; behold, all things are become new."
—II COR. 5:17

"PURITY OF HEART IS TO WILL ONE Thing." So goes the title of a devotional from another century. But the truth of it never grows old. When Jesus was asked to name life's greatest commandment, he recited this ancient law of his people, "Thou shalt love the Lord thy God with all thy heart."

Semiconversion constitutes one of life's major detriments to spiritual efficiency. The sharp youngster spoke for many of us when she and her parents were discussing the Sunday lesson. "But honey," said her mother, "don't you already have Jesus in your heart?" "I do, Mommy," came the answer,

"but sometimes he takes little trips." Almost anyone who has tried to be completely Christian will
feel a kinship with her problem.

When we look back down the road we have
come, most of us see evidence that we have not always been true to heaven's high call. In the path
behind us there are many little markers where we
buried some broken promises, shoveled the earth
on noble resolves, or laid our best to rest beneath
the tomb of good intent.

Always, the end result is the same. In the life of
the Kingdom there are no bargain counters. We
never get maximum results for minimum surrender. "We are his workmanship," and God in
his all-wise wisdom has decreed that his plan is
a full-time plan for full-time people.

Our Two-Part Creation

The problems of spiritual dedication are com-
pounded when we recognize our existence on two
levels. In the subchambers there may be trouble-
makers that steal our time and sap our energy.

We are fortunate to live in a day when brilliant
men are able to analyze the human mind and tell
us where we ail. In consultation they can ferret out
the real culprits and set us free to be at our best.

Wherever such aid is prescribed, we should accept it as another gift of God's good grace.

But professional psychiatry is out of range for many moderns. Too often the limited number of trained experts, or limited income, or prejudice, or distance, or human failures of both doctor and patient place this kind of help too far out for us.

Yet here again the Christian gospel shows its genius. It offers its all to any son of the Father who is prepared to receive it with purity of heart. We may have done badly on our own. We may have lived all our lives in partial commitment. There may be hangers-on in the back room hidden from our eyes. Yet for all these sad facts the promise holds: "If any man be in Christ, he is a new creature: old things are passed away; behold, all things become new."

Early Memories

"Accepting Christ" may not be as simple as it sounds for some of us. Consciously we may give him our all, but the subconscious roots must also be severed. He may know us fully, but sometimes he cannot do his best in us until we too know why we act as we do, how we got this way, and what caused our inner tensions.

One good place to start the search for hidden

trouble is in our childhood recollections. If we ask him, Christ will give us deeper insight to our background troubles than ever we have had before. He may guide us to people who themselves have recovered from the prison house of immaturity. We may be led to books which can assist us in self-analysis.

The early stages of our growth are important to the full understanding of our problems. The first time we discovered that someone didn't like us; the day we were caught cheating; the teacher who punished us unfairly; life's most embarrassing memory—all of these left their marks on our subconscious. Great is the day when we can face these things, turn them over to the Lord, and hear him say, "All things are become new."

It is gospel truth that Christ can redeem our lives from destruction and restore the years of "pestilence, blasting, mildew, locust, or . . . caterpiller." But before "old things are passed away" in some of us, he requires an inner honesty which faces facts and knows where the problems are.

Here again, it is important for us to remember that our Lord is courteous. He stands at our heart door and knocks. He waits and knocks again. But he never crashes our privacy. The latch is on the inside and his coming in is up to us.

But once he has made his entrance, there'll be some changes made. We have seen that his holiness is not content with things as he finds them. He turns over the rug and looks for forgotten dust. He insists on doing this room over and throwing away that trash. He is the great disturber. He is a renovater. He will be Lord if we ask him, but only on his terms. He makes things new to suit his taste.

But, when we have let him have his way, he pours in his freshness.

Results of the Inner Redemption

When he comes with all his newness we will experience *new powers of concentration*. Whereas our old self had been serving many masters, known and unknown, now the new Lord of life sets us free to center down in singleness of heart. In this experience we find ourselves increasingly able to do one thing at a time. This is inevitable. By his power to redeem, he breaks the clutches of our old time stealers and cuts us loose to do each single job and do it well. Likewise those scattering voices pressuring us to consider things still undone will quiet themselves in his companionship. He gives us to know that "For everything there is a season" and our "times are in thy hands" (R.S.V.).

When his inner newness becomes real we will feel *new staying power*. Jesus said, "He that endureth to the end shall be saved." This finishing stuff of Christ is a crying need for most of us. Some unknown humorist put his hand on our pulse when he revised one of Longfellow's poems:

Toiling—rejoicing—sorrowing,
So I my life conduct;
Each morning sees some task begun
Each evening sees it chucked.

That sounds a familiar drum. It is easy to make good beginnings. But the week doesn't end on Wednesday and the measurements aren't taken at the halfway point. Our failure to stay with it has cost us many a victory. On our record too may be houses we started to build but did not finish. It is this power to keep on keeping on which the indwelling Christ provides when our lives have been uncluttered for his operation.

New freedom from fear is another gift of the Spirit's inner grace. His truth puts us at liberty. The former neuroses which stole our strength and took up our time will slowly starve when he lives in us. He cuts these robbers off at the inner feedbox and uses our energy to nourish better ends.

As we learn to live in his calm, he takes the ghosts of yesterday and puts these too in "the former things [which] are passed away." Those positive fears, which constitute his alarm system in our hearts, are now in his control. He'll use them when we need them, take them back when they have done their work, and stand by with his wisdom to show us the difference between fears that are good and fears that are evil.

New Knowledge of Self for New Knowledge of Him

Alcoholics Anonymous, the dynamic organization that has been the organ of new hope to thousands of out-of-control lives, has a phrase which is a vital part of its recovery process: "We made a decision to turn our will and our lives over to the care of God as we understood him."

This touches on a great truth. We must begin where we are. Because we are composed of both "awareness" and "unawareness," many of us do not fully understand immediately all that is involved in total Christian commitment.

But Christ is the great meeter of problems in their present condition. When we tell him that we want him to make us new in him, he brings his insight to our blindness.

Yet these new visions never come easy. Anyone who has ever tried to live under the new lordship knows that it takes all there is of him all of the time. We do not live in the spirit "give your heart to Jesus and he will do it all." We may begin our life with Christ in any moment, but for most of us to become true Christians is more of a process than a single act. Yet this need not discourage us. So it will take a lifetime? All the more reason to begin at once.

God sent his Son to set us free from sin and guide us to an ever fuller knowledge of the Kingdom within. For us then self-understanding is not a matter of techniques and systems, methods of analysis and schools of psychology. These are important and we will do all within our power to understand the particular contribution which each can make to our enlightenment.

But for us the greatest single contribution to self-understanding is to better understand that we are made in the image of God. Each day we pray for new insights. By this prayer we understand more of the destruction our self-centered living has wrought. Yet by this prayer we also learn more of his power to reconstruct.

As we open our inner rooms to more of his coming, we will catch new visions of his ability to make right what we have made wrong. And in this vision we will see a Lord who asks only one thing—that we daily bring new understandings of our weakness to our new understandings of his greatness. His piercing light in the deep places of our souls shows us what we are, and this may seem all to the bad when we view it alone. But it also shows us what we were meant to be in his love, and this will be all to the good. When this new knowledge of ourselves meets with our new knowledge of him, we are touched with new power for new uses in his plan.

Affirmation V

I Plan for the Future but I Enjoy Today

Looking Ahead and Living Now

"For which of you, intending to build a tower, sitteth not down first, and counteth the cost, whether he have sufficient to finish it. Lest haply, after he hath laid the foundation, and is not able to finish it, all that behold it begin to mock him, saying, This man began to build, and was not able to finish."

—LUKE 14:28-30

"Take therefore no thought for the morrow: for the morrow shall take thought for the things of itself."

—MATT. 6:34

MODERN LIFE HAS A WAY OF CON-fusing us at some points. On the one hand, it says, "Plan ahead! Look to tomorrow! Press on!" But the same voices of the world seem to be saying "Live today! This is the hour! Now! Now! Now!"

48

Faced with this problem, we turn to Christ for guidance. But when we examine the today and tomorrow teachings of the Master, we find what appears to be a contradiction.

What can a disciple do when one word of his leader seems to refute another? One solution is to move away from the immediate statements and look to their backgrounds. When we do this with these two directives, we find that what looked like opposites are actually two branches from the same root. And the root is to commit all time, this day and the days ahead, for his use.

The Right Way to Look Ahead

As we review the Lukan word on wise tower builders who plan ahead, we find an interesting setting. When Jesus gave these words, he was on his way to Jerusalem. Crowds were following him. They were increasing in size and excitement. They looked beyond him down the road and saw him on a throne in command of their earthly kingdom. They were counting on sharing the glory of a restored Israel. Their fond dream was coming alive.

But Jesus' eyes were focused on an eternal dream of the Father himself. Whereas they were looking to tomorrow for themselves, he was look-

49

ing into the future that he might better accomplish the will of God.

This then is the teaching: *Whoever looks to tomorrow with an eye to heaven's plan has discovered the right way to look ahead!*

There are evidences that Jesus himself planned certain events prior to their happening. A careful reading of the prelude to the Lord's Supper indicates that he pre-arranged some matters. There are those who hold that Christ had clairvoyant powers to see each detail of the future. Did he know that as the hour of the Passover drew near there would be a man with a pitcher of water standing at a particular spot in a particular village? (See Mark 14:13; Luke 22:10.) Did he know that this man would go to a certain room and that preparations would be made there? Or had Jesus carefully worked out every move in this dangerous hour? Was he here telling the disciples what signals he had agreed would be used by his men and the man with whom he had planned?

At the moment of his triumphal entry, related in all three of the Synoptic Gospels (Matt. 21; Mark 11; Luke 19), was the colt tied at that particular spot because Christ had made arrangements? Were the words of the owner, "Why do ye loose him?" and the reply of the disciples, "Because the Lord hath need of him," part of a pre-directed code? Some of us do not think that it takes anything away from our Lord to believe that these events were carefully planned by his own habit of thinking in advance.

This has something to say to us. Schedules, programs, careful consideration of the road ahead, these need not crush the joy from our lives. It is true that they will bear on us if they are designed for self-promotion. But they will bear us up if we plan them for sacred purposes. The fact stands that there is nothing evil about looking to tomorrow if we do this with an eye to the needs of our Lord. Prudence and forethought are always good when they are Christ-directed from within.

Full Enjoyment of This Hour

Yet planning ahead has some definite dangers. Unless we are alert here we may find ourselves in the unhappy ranks of the continual "postponers." As we stand in this line we hear familiar phrases.

"When we get the house paid for, then we can relax—Next month things will be less stringent. Then we can really contribute to good causes— The first of the week is a better time to start that diet— If we made our reforms on January first, we could more easily measure our progress—Some

51

other day we will write that letter—When we have a little bit more in the bank, then we will spend time with our wife and family—Next year! Some day! Tomorrow!"

Such things as these must surely have been on the firing line of Jesus' teaching to "take therefore no thought for the morrow."

A study of the Greek meaning of these words will help to clear the seeming contradiction in our Lord's advice. Some of the modern versions are nearer to the original intent when they translate the verse, "Do not be anxious about tomorrow" (R.S.V.), or "So do not worry about tomorrow" (Goodspeed).

When we view the passage in this light, we find the same basic principle applying in both Matthew and Luke. We look to the future that we may be at our best for God. We live today to the fullest because we are living this day with him.

We do well to note that Jesus' words about anxiety and tomorrow are set in a passage which deals with men and their material needs. Immediately preceding this teaching, Matthew sets down thoughts concerning treasures on earth and treasures in heaven. He follows this with the famous declaration, "Ye cannot serve God and mammon [riches]" (Matt. 6:24).

This is an unrelenting word. He does not say that it is inadvisable to serve God and riches. He says it cannot be done. It cannot be done for this reason—Christianity only works right when Christ is in first place!

It is a great day for us when we realize that life is for only one thing—living God's way! Our Lord came to show us how to do this. He wants us to know that we must think about food and clothing but not first! We must think about tomorrow—but not first! We must "seek first the kingdom and his righteousness" and let him add as he wills to tomorrow and today.

This is the basic of basics in all our planning. We are alive this moment and this moment is for one thing. This very moment is a holy moment. In this sacred now we can look to the days ahead without frenzy. The divine hand of our time master shapes the days ahead and this day, tomorrow's moments and this moment, each to its proper mold. If we are in communion with him, things will be what they should be tomorrow and they are what they should be right now.

When we open our hearts to his presence in full honesty, he comes to live his life in us and think his thoughts through us. Now our future is what it needs to be eternally. Now our present is alive with his glory.

All our time is for one thing. Always to the Christian safe planning for the future and full enjoyment of every hour depends on this: Are we using today and planning tomorrow for fuller companionship, better service, and more total commitment to the Lord whose we are and whom we serve?

Affirmation VI

I Do Not Attempt to Do It All

> "No!"
> *"And great multitudes came together to hear, and to be healed by him of their infirmities. And he withdrew himself into the wilderness, and prayed."*
>
> —LUKE 5:15-16

How could he go away when there were throngs to be blessed and bodies in need of his healing?

We cannot be sure of the answer. Perhaps he knew that the frenzied excitement of the throng was about to reach dangerous proportions. Maybe he withdrew because his reserves were depleted to the danger mark. Did he feel that to give from a bleached-out soul would be detrimental to the Kingdom?

Whatever the reason, it is evident that he left something which needed doing.

Tending Our Own Business

"He withdrew himself into the wilderness and prayed" is balm for our soul when we are crushed by a false sense of responsibility. It has a healing sound if we tend at all toward rigid perfectionism. As we study the life of Christ, it seems to testify that our Creator does not expect us to do every good work which needs doing.

In another section, we will study the art of letting other people contribute their part to the Kingdom's handiwork. Here it suffices to note that no Christian can do all the good. True, we must love the world and have concern for its needs. But it is not our job to save it by ourselves. God is depending on us, but not on us entirely. Some things are outside the sphere of our divine assignment, and we take a mighty step forward when we sense this truth.

There is wisdom in the story of Grandpa's gate. It is an old tale with many versions. As the aged sage worked on his gate, the small boy approached with his inevitable question, "Whatcha' doin', Grandpa?" To which the fixer answered: "Laddy, there's five kinds of broken things in this old world. There's the kind which, when they are broken, no one can fix. There's them which, when they are broken, will fix themselves if we leave them alone. Then there's the kind which, when they are broken, somebody else has got to fix. There's also the kind which, when they're broken, only God can fix. And then, little man, there's the kind which when they are broken, I got to fix. That's what I'm doin', fixin' this gate!"

Because life is arranged as Grandpa says, one noise sure to be heard in the path of any saint is the sound of some things falling away. When we truly surrender to the way of Christ there comes the quiet assurance that some matters must wait for another time, or for other people, or for God alone. We are to tend to *our* business for him.

It goes without saying that this can be dangerous reasoning. But not to understand the truth of it may be even more dangerous to the Kingdom. The fact looms large and encouraging. Jesus did not heal them all. He did not go at the same pace all the time. He did not permit an audience to everyone.

We catch our breath when we read that he seemed, at least for a moment, to reject even his mother and brothers (Matt. 12:46-50) for his larger relationship to all the world. The obvious conclusion is that he could not do all things at once, and therefore he must do what God needed doing through him right then.

This is still good procedure. Our activities may become a frantic drive to nowhere unless we are rooted and grounded in the spiritual commitment which accepts each holy assignment as it comes and leaves the rest in the hands of God.

"No!" to the Already Done

Could it be that Christ walked away from the crying crowd beause he had already finished the heavenly assignment? Had he completed his part of that day's work in the Father's will?

Some of us could improve our efficiency if we would let the done be done. It was an astute young lady who observed: "No wonder I'm worn out! I do everything I do so many times. First I worry about doing it—then when I have done it, I do it over, worrying whether I did it right." If the promises of God are true, then we can trust him to build on what we have already done in co-operation with him. This is another reason why life with the Inner Presence is the life of peace. We plan with him. Then we work with him. Then we leave the finished product in his care. We move on to other work for him and give our best to this new calling. He will call us back to that which we have done before if there is some added contribution he needs from us.

"No!" to others is sometimes a must for Christian efficiency at its Christly best. But so also is "No!" to ourselves.

"No!" Today for God's Tomorrow

A study of the context of Luke 5:16 indicates that Jesus may have withdrawn himself in preparation for the initial appearance of his opposition. From this first meeting there were to develop battle lines which intensified to bitter hatred. Did he sense the coming of thunderheads on his horizon? Did he have some inner warning that he had best make ready for the road ahead? To these questions comes the same monotonous answer, "We do not know." But it does appear that his "No!" of this particular day may have been getting him ready for the "Yes!" of God's tomorrow.

Efficiency in the management of time may wait on our recognition that we can never please all people. Unless we aim to please Christ first we may say "Yes!" to too many requests because we care too much what the world thinks. Overbusyness could be a telltale pointer to uncommitted areas in our hearts. Those everybody-says you're-the-only-person-for-it lurings have an appalling appeal.

When we find ourselves enmeshed in too much doing, this may be a signal that our dedication has been to less than the best. At times like this we are more likely to need wilderness and prayer than acclaim and the world's good will.

Still another subtle danger is that we may stack up our calendar in the future just because it is far away. There are some subtle reasons why we succumb to invitations two months distance more easily than two days ahead. Most of us operate under the delusion that we will soon have big chunks of time with nothing important on the agenda. But when we see the future through Christ's eyes we know that six months from next Monday is the same as today. It too is a sacred hour, reserved for divine use, and we do well to refer these requests of the distant schedule to our Lord. He alone can tell us how all the present and the future are to be used to his glory.

Further study of the Gospels reveals that Jesus often withdrew himself for spiritual communion when the crowds were seeking him. Our tendency is the opposite when we are running our lives alone. We are prone to throw ourselves increasingly into high gear as the demands increase. With banners flying we charge on. "The mail must go through!" But before we know it the horse is spent

60

and its rider done. A firm refusal, when it is heaven-directed, may be the rein which brings us to a screeching halt for Christ's sake.

"Yes!" can be a word replete with blessing. But so also can "No!" Rightly used, it is an efficiency expert of the highest order. This is always true when it is the voice of Christ from deep within.

Affirmation VII

I Will Make Friends with Divine
Interruptions

Opportunity in Each Intrusion

*"And Jesus arose, and followed him,
and so did his disciples. And, behold,
a woman, which was diseased with an
issue of blood twelve years, came behind him, and touched the hem of
his garment: For she said within her-
self, If I may but touch his garment,
I shall be whole. But Jesus turned
him about, and when he saw her, he
said, Daughter, be of good comfort;
thy faith hath made thee whole. And
the woman was made whole from that
hour."*

—MATT. 9:19-22

JESUS WAS IN A HURRY. A CERTAIN
ruler had come pleading for his daughter's life.
Would he come at once? This was an emergency
of the gravest sort and the Master of time set out
without delay. But here in this most urgent mis-

sion comes the inevitable problem—what can be done with the interruptions?

We have been witness to the Christ who said "No!" where we would be prone to say "Yes!" Now we see him giving the "Yes!" to what looks like the moment for a justified "No!"

On his way to handle one crucial matter, Christ takes time for another. As he moves toward the restoration of one life, he halts his urgent going to put the finishing touches on another. Always about our Lord there is this sensitiveness to divine guidance at unexpected times and in surprising places.

When we put our ear down to the Gospels we hear echoes of this same thing repeated often in the Master's affairs. Mark seems particularly sensitive to the checks and hindrances in Jesus' way. He cites such incidents as, "There came one running" (Mark 10:17), "And when they had found him, they said unto him, All men seek for thee" (Mark 1:37), and "There were many coming and going, and they had no leisure so much as to eat" (Mark 6:31). These are revealing. Not only do they give evidence of the press and pull in our Lord's daily activity, but his reactions furnish us material for serious meditation.

When the man came running, Jesus stopped

his own going and asked, "What would ye that I should do for you?" (Mark 10:36.) When the schedule became so jammed that even their meals were crowded out, he hurried the disciples into a boat and moved off for a desert place. (See Mark 6:32.) But this attempt at solitude broke down because the people saw him leave and rushed around the lake to meet him. We observe now a true Christly reaction. Mark tells us, "Jesus, when he came out, saw much people, and was moved with compassion toward them, because they were as sheep not having a shepherd: and he began to teach them many things." (Mark 6:34.)

When we ponder his reaction we sense that back of each obstruction to his schedule there seems to be an attunement to heaven's direction.

As we have seen, sometimes he said "No!" and so must we. But at other times he paused to take up a little child, or heal a long-forgotten lame man, or feed a hungry multitude. And so must we be ready when God calls.

Christian Flexibility

One of the marks of true Christian greatness will be a certain "interruptibility." This life has an elastic quality. It is equipped with expansion points. Already containing many interests, such a soul has room for one more real need if it comes from higher up.

We have observed that our heavenly Father never gives us too much to do. Men will. We assign ourselves an overload, but never the Lord. He knows what he wants from each of us, and there is plenty of time in his day for things essential to his plan. We do him grave injustice when we fall into the habit of compulsive overwork. We sin when we pressure out his wishes for assignments that have not been filtered through divine judgment. Self-centered scheduling that wants it our way and ours alone is far different from setting up a plan with the Inner Presence as our guide.

Perhaps a real assist to Christian flexibility would be to allow some time for unforeseen interruptions. The Christian who seeks to be at his best for holy purposes may need to discipline himself in the art of the early start. He will plan his schedule with a stretch factor. He will aim to have work ready before the given deadline. Certain of these simple techniques may mean much in the release of personal tension. They may also be a manifold improvement in the soul tools we offer our Lord for his use.

One sure proof that we are growing up in Christ is the increasing capacity to endure these interruptions. We can test for spiritual progress by this measurement: Are we learning the art of the abrupt stop? Perhaps so common a matter as our relationship with our family can give us the assist we need to master this matter. "Just a minute!" "Someday when I have more time!" "When I get this done I'll read to you!" "Can't you wait a few seconds?" may be necessary on some occasions. But they may not. If we are in tune with the Master's spirit, he may show us that this particular time is the occasion for another quick quit.

If Christ is truly living his life in us there is likely to be a new serenity in our activities and a fresh new graciousness in all our contacts with the rest of the world.

Gratitude for Life's Intrusions

One of my jobs in college was running an elevator. There is no work which calls for "interruptibility" quite like this—up and down, never going anywhere, just doing the same thing over and over again. Second floor, then first, then basement. Now some infuriated soul leans hard on the bell at seventh. Endless interruptions and looks which slay the soul are very much a part of life in this employment. It is good to be kind to those who run elevators.

But then one month I was shifted to the night force. Now in the long hours it was a matter of dull sitting. This was the lonesome shift and it was maddening with solitude. How glad I was then for an interruption.

It is true that "All men seek for thee," "There came one running," and "They had no leisure so much as to eat," are reflections of a serious problem with the Master of time. But their absence might have indicated some real problems of even more concern.

This is for us. The doctor who never had a call at midnight; the mother whose constantly intruding little one might suddenly be taken from her; the businessman whose office should cease to be a parade of seekers after this and that—all of us, without encroachment, would be a somber lot.

In another chapter we will see that the truest joy of the Lord comes in being of real use to God's plan. If we are really maturing with the Inner Director, we will learn to give thanks when he calls for our services at all hours or any time.

"Man's Interruptions Are God's Opportunities"

This old proverb will hang on a prominent wall in any Christ-committed soul. When we have dedicated our lives to his use, we are brought one day to this light: *On numerous occasions the inter-rupter is more important than the interrupted.*

As we study the ninth chapter of Matthew we ask: How can a woman with issue take precedence over a girl who lies gripped in the clutches of death? No human knows the answer to this one. The same truth applies to us. Only God can tell where we are needed most this minute or tomorrow at nine o'clock. True, he can work his purpose out eventually without our little efforts. But our lives are his equipment when we are living in committment to his will. It is an awesome thought that our feet may be his shortcuts, our hands may save him time, our thoughts may be the circuits by which he makes contact with his own.

Whether it is one of those long interruptions when we are put flat on our back to think life over, or a jangling phone just when we have settled down in the big chair to read the news, or a morning when our cherished plan for that day is utterly devastated before one hour is past, we have learned a great secret when we live in this faith: There are no interruptions if we are in accord with the Lord.

Some items will still be unimportant. If this is an intrusion to which we must say "No!" he will give us the grace to say it right. If we are letting him use us, he can call us back from this break to deeper dedication.

When we are living the Christ-centered life, it is a foregone conclusion that there will be interruptions. The life of dedication is never regulated by our preferences. It is the heaven-used life where he, living in us, draws his own to himself for holy reasons.

Here comes that man again!
The phone is ringing!
There is a knock at our door!
People and questions, requests and things!

What must we do? For those who seek first to do the mission of the Lord, there is one true test which must be put to every inroad and each intrusion: Is this the Inner Presence calling his own?

Affirmation VIII

I Will Be Courteous of Others' Time

Their Time Is God's Time Too

> *"Treat men just as you wish them to treat you."*
>
> —LUKE 6:31 (GOODSPEED)

GOODSPEED REPHRASES THE FAMOUS Golden Rule from negative to positive. The Christian ethic is like that. Jesus changed the laws of life from "Thou shalt not" to "This do, and thou shalt live." In the ancient codes of conduct, righteousness was often judged by refraining from certain taboos. But for the Lord of life, this was not enough. He was never content with disciples who tested their goodness by a minimum of badness. Always, examination of the committed life will include the way our lives affect the lives of others.

A sensitive approach to the Christian use of time is sure to consider our habits and the people around us. Here we can measure ourselves at several places.

Their Time and Our Hands Off

We have noted that our Lord does not expect us to remake the world by our own little selves. The immaculate mother who must do everything about the house because she can do it better; the meddling foreman who hasn't learned to keep hands off when he has given assignments to others; the perfectionist executive who delegates work but never cuts his subordinates loose to use their own imagination—these, and all of us who hang on too tight to the other fellow's share, might experience a bright new blessing if we lived by the Golden Rule. This everyday law of our everyday Lord could be a healing potion to the golden ulcer building up in our own tense selves. It might also save us from frustrating the holy designs of the Lord in others. Life for the Christ-centered is never solo 100 per cent of the time. Our Father's business is a matter of teamwork.

Before we can be free of false drives we may need to face this truth: Our heavenly Father has no favorites. Though we may be wonderfully wrought, so is everyone else in the sense that God has dreams for all his own. He loves his children alike. He has a plan for each of them. When we know this truth it will be easier to practice the

71

Golden Rule that gives men room to grow for heaven's development of their talents.

Anyone who seriously studies the life of Christ will see that this master of men used other men. He did not attend to all that needed doing. He sent the disciples into the village to inquire for food and lodging. He directed them to the city to prepare the Upper Room. He asked them to find food for feeding the multitude. He chose disciples and trained them until they could go out by twos to preach, teach, bless, and heal. They must learn to go on without him. They were his hope. They were his co-creators of the Kingdom.

When Christ lives in us with his gentle touch on other heartstrings; when he shows us where to take hold and where to keep hands off; when he is tending his business in our business, we will feel the pressure slacken, and in this loosening up of our false hold we, and those who deal with us, may find new access to his peace.

Their Time and Our Tardiness

Another positive test for the positive Golden Rule in us may be at the point of punctuality.

In a fast-growing company, the board of directors has adopted this interesting procedure. Their biweekly meeting is held on Monday afternoon at

72

four o'clock. Promptly on the hour, doors to the board room are closed. A porter stands at the entrance with what is known as "The tardy box." Before a latecomer is given entrance he must deposit here an amount equal to ten cents per tardy minute mutiplied by the number of men who have made it on the hour. If there are fifteen directors within the chamber, each minute delayed will cost the dilatory member one dollar and fifty cents; ten minutes, fifteen dollars. The only exceptions are those who have excused themselves to the secretary at least thirty minutes prior to the meeting's start.

This unusual cure for an ancient nuisance might cause considerable stir in some quarters. But those in charge of the company affairs recommend it as a quick cure for the latecomers. (It may be of interest to note that at the year's end the most punctual member names his favorite charity to receive "the kitty.")

Most of us would be glad to settle for much less than ten cents multiplied by the number of minutes we have been kept waiting. But if the tables were turned and we were charged for our own lagging, the wages of sin might balance the books.

Yet for the Christian this technique seems no more than fair. Since all our time is the heavenly

Father's, then all our associates' time is also his. It is an awesome fact that whenever we are inconsiderate of those about us we may sin against the Lord's plan for other lives.

Their Time and Our Inner Listener

One more excellent testing place for use of our time and of other people's time is at the point of listening. Those who are serious about living by the Golden Rule will study its application to everyday conversation.

Much of the gospel record is given to Jesus' talk, but throughout these biographies of the Lord there are generous sprinklings of such phrases as "When Jesus heard that, . . ." "As soon as Jesus heard the word," "When Jesus heard these things," "And when Jesus heard it, he answered him." We get a fuller understanding of his work with people when we tune our ear to his frequent questions: "Dost thou?" "Wilt thou?" "Hast thou?"

Some of us need this art of our Lord for the time we spend with others. Often we sit on the edge of the sofa and fidget nervously until the other fellow has finished with his story. We wait for an opening. Or sometimes we don't wait. When he takes a breath, we seize the floor to tell what

74

we heard about the matter, or who *is* going to win, or *our* opinion of the business before us.

Christ was not like this. The scripture accounts show him strong on the listening side. When the Inner Presence guides our life we may see that folks don't need to hear us nearly so much as they need to hear themselves. This is why our voice, which rings like a bell to us, is likely to sound like the caw of a crow to the man who needs to express himself. This is especially important as we grow and advance in our particular field. Unless we guard it, the higher up life's ladder we go, the more we usurp the conversational patterns. We may be lured into believing that people want to know all about us. They don't! They want us to know about them.

Most of us cannot manage this alone. Only the Golden Rule of Christ living in us can gradually teach us that the ministry of the ear may be more vital than the ministry of the mouth. If we ask him to, and mean it, the Lord of true quiet can bring us out of the hypnotic state where we have been lulled by our own voice. Always, Christly love knows how to be silent.

A careful observation of Jesus' listening indicates that at times he also heard things which were not spoken. Things unsaid sometimes indicate a soul that cries within. It behooves us to develop Christian ears both for the said and the unsaid.

This is a big order. Here then, as always, the loadstone in this building of the soul is to open our hearts to the Holy Spirit and ask him to take over our hearing deep within. He will teach us how to filter the words, the sounds, the said and the unsaid, through his spirit. Only he can tell us when people need a "word fitly spoken" in his spirit from our tongue. He alone can tell us when to keep still, or when to withdraw if others do not want to talk, or if they want to talk to someone other than ourselves.

The Rule Behind the Golden Rule

It can readily be seen by what we have said that to treat men as we wish them to treat us is a major challenge. But behind this Golden Rule there must be more than sheer determination to rid our lives of selfishness. If our interest in others is a fabrication which we put on for the party, if it is not genuine but only for the use we can make of it, people will soon be wise to our insincerity.

Therefore, the rule behind the Golden Rule must be the rule of true Christian love. When Christ lives in us, we need not simulate love, nor work so hard at it. Instead we love the world with

76

an infinite tenderness beyond our own capacity. This is not a matter of speaking if we happen to feel like speaking. Nor is smiling at strategic times or putting out a warm hand at propitious moments. It is the deepest depths of the divine reaching out, which has as its aim the redemption of all society.

There will be some real surprises when Christ takes over our contacts with others. Be he black, white, tan, yellow, green with envy, red with rage, each one is our brother in the Lord.

This is the Christian's faith. Each to all and each to each is bound in holy creation. Christ gave his life for this truth. Even when men refused to return his love, when they nailed him up in rejection, he insisted that this was the way. Men were sons of one Father and he would love on in dying testimony that love is the final winner.

We may not sit at the peace tables of the nations. In our human weakness we may not be able to convince others that our love is true. Perhaps we cannot even relieve all the quarreling in the family or in the neighborhood. But we can do this: We can let Christ live in us and beam his inner light to every soul.

His love at work in us works manifold blessings to lover and loved alike. His love is like a branch on which the weary bird can rest. It is like a hammock in the shade at the end of a hot day. His love is a light on a dark night. It is a hand which leads us and others out of the jungle to the broad highway.It casts out fear. It bathes the soul in good will and leaves a feeling of peace.

Furthermore, this love begets additional love because his love always seeks further ways to express itself. Love is never bored. It constantly plans happy surprises and lives in expectancy of their occurrence. It rejoices in others' rejoicing and plunges itself daily in the streams of gladness. Because it makes life good for others, it is never a stranger to goodness. Without fail, Christian love creates a climate where time and all life's business can be at its best.

To live in his love is to live by the rule behind the Golden Rule. When we have opened our hearts all the way to his presence, we become true citizens of that sacred world where all souls have harmony, and our lives have harmony, because we are in harmony with him.

Affirmation IX

I Will Live by the Secrets of Christian Joy

The Efficiency of Gladness

"These things have I spoken unto you, that my joy might remain in you, and that your joy might be full."

—JOHN 15:11

THE NEW PREACHER SAT IN GRANDMA Davidson's kitchen. He had just preached his initial sermon in his first church. The little country congregation had "borne up well" under the offering of this untried seminary graduate. Long years of amateur gospel presentation had given these people a saving callousness of soul to match their weather-beaten faces. They had "toughed it out" through many an embryonic shepherd whom they were proud to make ready for what the world called "more important pulpits."

On this particular sabbath the neophyte pastor sat eating Grandma Davidson's fried chicken as he took in her comments. She, like her well-worn neighbors, had listened intently to the gospel offering that morning and she was downcast, but she was not destroyed. Wasn't that a faint gleam in the young man's eye? Maybe she could do something about this.

Of course these boys from the seminary were weary with study and heavy-laden with the importance of their labors in the Kingdom. Most of them were hungry, like this one, but they might take some advice with their victuals. This was her part. Her theology wasn't learned from books, but she knew some things he should know, and he never forgot the way she put it:

"We were hopin' for a preacher," she began, "who'd know the other side of the Lord Jesus. We've had our plenty of doom. That's part of the truth, but it ain't all. I always felt like the true comin' of the Lord in us sinners must be somethin' like it is when the sun breaks through on a gloomy day. We know there's a judgment comin'. The likes of you has been preachin' and scoldin' and tellin' us that for thirty years. But I always thought someday some preacher around here would know that some of the gospel is glad tidings. I hope I'm not just a meddlin' old lady but, like I said, I should think studyin' that out would do wonders for you. And Law-me, what it wouldn't do for us!"

Twenty times the earth has circled the sun since

she presented this lesson in glad tidings. And in my studies I have discovered that she was right.

More than two hundred times the Bible uses forms of the word "joy." In one version of the New Testament there are sixty-three associations of Jesus and that word. Five times each the gospel writers employ "cheer," "merry," and "laugh," as they tell their stories. "Glad" makes seven appearances, while the verb "rejoice" is repeated on eighteen occasions. As we pore over the words which Christ spoke and the words spoken about him, the truth shapes itself. In order to describe him these terms had to be used repeatedly for an honest picture. It is true that Jesus was "a man of sorrows, and acquainted with grief." This is well to know. It means that he is touched with the feeling of our infirmities," and he understands how it feels when life is hard. But we do our Lord a grave injustice if we keep only this side of the Master before us.

He longed for us to be glad. One day he said to his disciples, "These things have I spoken unto you, that my joy might remain in you, and that your joy might be full."

Examination of the context from which he said these words clearly shows that Christian joy is no chance prize to the lucky winners of some celestial giveaway. There may be lesser wellsprings, but a careful reading of the chapter will uncover these twin fountains of the joy of the Lord:

1. Full consciousness of God's love.
2. Full obedience to his will.

First Wellspring of Christian Joy: The Love of God

Child psychologists know that the greatest gift parents can give their children is a solid foundation of love on which to build their lives. Experience proves that a mother and father who love their family, who love their neighbors and the world, who love each other and aren't afraid to let this be known to little minds, are making the best single contribution which can be made toward healthy maturing.

The same thing applies in the realm of the spirit. We never grow up in full Christian stature until we have a right idea of God. It is no accident that John's words on full joy follow on the undried ink of a foregoing charge: "Continue ye in my love" (John 15:9).

Jesus came to do many things for men. He came to show us what God is like, and in a very real sense the entire New Testament is commentary on that. It can be truly said that no teaching on things divine could possibly improve on the three-word capsule summary of I John 4:8: *"God is love!"*

Anyone who has ever grasped the significance of this fact, and lived by it, has found a sure source of Christian joy at its purest.

Joy, originating in the love of God, adds zest. It is an energizing quality because it sets us free to work at our maximum. It cuts us loose from many time-stealers which would tie us down in anxious fretting. It makes the load seem lighter and permits us fuller attention to things that count in the Father's plan.

But freedom from fear is not the only contribution here. When we truly comprehend God's love for us we will know the potent new powers which come with thanksgiving. Always, the Christian's inner atmosphere is vibrant with appreciation.

That person who has been lost in the woods, or has stood alone at night wondering which way to turn for safety; who has felt his heart panic, or has sensed the desolation of going it alone—that person can recall vividly how his soul leaped high with gratitude when he heard someone calling his name.

This is what it means to really sense the amazing

grace of God's love. The heart that hears his call will be glad for many things. But above all this heart rejoices in the thrilling companionship that leads, directs, corrects, remakes, disciplines, yet is ever-loving with a holy concern for its own.

This is a certain test for the Indwelling Presence. When we are overcome with thanksgiving for life and everything it it, we can be sure that the Lord is not far away. When our prayers seem sometimes to be nothing but a repetition of the words "thank you," we can know that we are experiencing the Kingdom in our hearts.

Such a feeling as this pours new strength into our weariness. It steps up our efficiency by a tremendous lift of soul. It gives us the sense that we are using this particular moment for its original intent. We have quit wasting our energy because we are no longer trying to get God to work with us. We are working with him and in his work is our true joy.

Second Wellspring of Christian Joy:
The Will of God.

Augustine is reported to have said, "True joy is a serious matter." Christian gladness is all of that.

We have been wisely warned by the critics of modern religion that overemphasis on happiness can make a buffoonery of faith. Christianity is not for the creation of "Pollyanna" disciples. The number one reason for following Christ is not that we might be joyful. John puts the order right when he says, "I always do what pleases him." (John 8:29 Moffatt.) We do well also to ponder long before these words: "For even Christ pleased not himself" (Rom. 15:3).

It is wise to observe that both the verses which precede and follow Jesus' "These things have I spoken unto you, that my joy might remain in you" have to do with his commandments. He makes it clear that his joy comes from this source, and ours must derive at the same waters. The label here is *"Obedience!"*

The true joy which cuts us free from the world's clutter and sets us at liberty to do things right for God is always based on an intimate relationship with Christ *at his terms.*

It will be obvious to the thinking Christian that there is a vast difference between "peace-of-mind" religion and true "resurrection joy." The former tends to be only veneer. But the genuine gladness of the risen Christ within comes only to those who have shared his cross. Always a vital theology remembers that the somber dirge of Friday precedes the Easter song.

This is why "joy" and "fun," as we commonly refer to them, may be two entirely different things. Pleasure, as we measure it, and Christian contentment are often at opposite ends of the emotional pole. The liberating, life-giving joy of the Lord comes from letting him have what he wants in our hearts.

It is a great promise which Jesus makes when he says, "If ye abide in me, and my words abide in you, ye shall ask what ye will, and it shall be done unto you." It is easy for us to overlook the first little "if" of this promise. Limitless prayer, prayer which gets things done, prayer which pulsates with power is always the prayer of a human heart which has been one-willed with Christ. Jesus is trying to teach us by these words that, if we live in him as he lives in the Father, all of his divine energy will flow through us, and the amount of it we experience will depend upon the amount of our obedience. "He that abideth in me, and I in him, the same bringeth forth much fruit" is a sure thing. But when we truly understand him, we know that he means he will fill us with all the energy we need *to do his work*.

This is why the symbol of our faith must ever be that recurring cross. The Christian study of life's better management seems continually to bring us back to Gethsemane and a wooden beam on a desolate hill.

To anyone who understands the gospel, there comes a tremendous awe at what he did for us. But we do him wrong if we stand gazing at his gift to us and fail to knuckle down to this: *The Cross is also a symbol of something we must do for him.* We never see it to our full salvation until we recognize its penetrating call to yield our wishes to his wishes.

Every day, all day, his limitless concern surrounds us. He longs to use us and share himself with us. Every moment and each act is for our response to divine love. Only in this atmosphere of God loving us and us loving him can we find full joy. Only in this commitment do we become true stewards of all his time.

Affirmation X

All My Time Belongs to God

The Sacrament of Every Second

"Whether therefore ye eat, or drink, or whatsoever ye do, do all to the glory of God."

—I COR. 10:31

THERE IS A LOVELY LEGEND WHICH centers about the building of a great cathedral. When the project began, heaven's director of church construction announced a grand contest. Upon completion of the cathedral, the Lord would award a rare prize to that person who had made the most significant contribution to the finished edifice. It was expected that the decision would be accepted in good faith. There would be no explanation. God could do no wrong.

Considerable speculation followed the initial announcement. Who would be the favored winner? Wasn't the architect a prime possibility? Or the contractor? Might it be one of the craftsman who did rare work in glass, gold, iron, or brass? Could it be a sculptor? Or perhaps the head stone-master? Maybe it would be the carpenter assigned to that intricate grill above the altar? Throughout the development, each one did his best, and the result was such a masterpiece as had never been seen throughout the land.

But at the moment of high anticipation when the winner was announced, imagine the surprise. The recipient proved to be an old peasant woman who daily carried fodder to the ox that pulled the marble for the masons.

It is a winsome tale, told in varied versions, but all of them are good because they touch on a deep truth. God alone knows what counts for him and which deed done has the purest meaning in his eternal plan.

When we understand this truth, we see the reason for another steady beat throughout the Word of God. The Bible continually reminds us that all of life is holy. Our heavenly Father fashioned the world and everything in it. Because this is true, each act has implications beyond our comprehension. The more we steep ourselves in scripture, the more surely this truth adds up. "Whether therefore ye eat, or drink, or whatsoever ye do, do all to the glory of God" (I Cor. 10:31) is only one of numerous challenges to complete Christ-centeredness. "In *all* thy ways acknowledge him, and he shall direct thy paths." (Prov. 3:6.) "In *everything* by prayer and supplication with thanksgiving let your requests be made known unto God." (Phil. 4:6.) "Christ *is* all, and *in* all." (Col. 3:11.)

We have unlocked another secret to mature Christian management when we understand this truth and live by it.

God—*Always There and Always Interested*

Some wag has written an interesting poem:

> Executives are hard to see
> Their costly time I may not waste;
> I make appointments nervously
> And talk to them in haste.
> But any time of night or day,
> In places suitable or odd,
> I seek and get without delay
> An interview with God.

The accessability of our heavenly Father is one of life's richest blessings to those who know him intimately. There is no battery of secretaries, no labyrinth of protocol, no thumbing through little black books, no unwinding of red tape before we may come to the Lord who made us and longs to share each need of our lives. It is hard for us with

90

our finite minds to grasp the infinite interest with which God attends our ways.

As we study the life of Christ, we see many incidents which testify to God's limitless concern. We observe Jesus sitting by a well in weariness. Comes now a woman to draw water. We, in our finite vision might say, "This is a chance meeting." Yet from this contact, the woman is redeemed and "many more" from her witness are drawn to Christ. (See John 4.) The serious reader, when he recognizes the full impact of such a story, cannot but pray that his driblets of time may be to God's glory.

When we think it through, it has to be this way. So much of our time is taken up with things that seem like trivia. Life does have to be lived. For most of us, hands cannot be forever folded in prayer. Someone must get Sally to her dental appointment. Bobby does need to make it to school before the tardy bell. Husbands do require clean shirts for a good impression. There are luncheon appointments and letters to write, guests to receive and phones to answer, contracts to sign and dishes to do, meetings to attend and hose to mend, sales to make, lessons to study, lawns to mow, screen doors to fix. These all are so much a part of life that our only hope is to make all these a part of devotional living.

It is precisely at this point that the Christian gospel again reveals its genius. "All to the glory of God" living recognizes that there are no vacuums of disinterest in our heavenly Father's love. It means that he does care where we buy our meat and how we drive our car. He is there when we discuss the new market with the vice-president and when we smile at the child in the street. There are no places and no time-crannies where the spirit of Christ cannot permeate to bless, provided we let him be the Lord of every moment.

This attitude toward our time will not pressure us into a red-necked frenzy which never rests. That delightful feeling that we have nothing to do may be exactly what he has created in us right now for his later use. The Indwelling Presence is perfectly capable of standing us on our feet or of putting us on our backs. We will use these moments too for the fullness of his love.

Perhaps we will need to meditate on the frequent fact that Jesus did much during the night or in those early hours of the morning before most of his world was awake. Sleeplessness may be neurotic but so may too much time in bed. Does he want us to add more minutes to our day by adding more waking hours? Each of us must decide these things individually in prayerful attention to the inner voice. He cannot want us dragging through the day with half enough sleep in our reservoir. But have we shut him out of our hearts by slumber when we should be up and doing?

We may need other revisions in our attitude toward the day's activities. We will be alert to use the time scraps that once we wasted. We will recognize that many fine things can be done with minutes, which soon add up to hours and days. This sense of every day holiness brings us continually back to the inescapable verity: *Our days are not for doing, they are for being in right relationship to him.*

Calm and Holy Urgency

This being in right relationship creates in us an amazing mixture of heavenly quiet and heavenly imperative.

Jesus said, "My Father worketh hitherto, and I work." We should notice the order. Most of us have given at least part of our lives in attempts at luring the Lord to come our way. When Christ lifts the curtain on our inner motives, we sometimes find ourselves well down the road ahead of his presence. Why doesn't he hurry it up? There is so much to do, so many people, so little time.

Yet this is not straight thinking and we know it. The divine "must" of the gospel is never a rush job. It moves at a steady pace, or it sits by the side of the road to wait on further orders. We need not whip up enthusiasm for more doing. Life is his and we are his. Time is his and every second of our living is his to work his work at his cadence in our hearts.

That was a wise word the angel gave to the women at the tomb on Easter morning. They had come worried about a stone that was already rolled away. Like many of our problems, unbeknown to them, God had been at work on their great need. We too can live in the true glory of Easter when we get the angel's sequence, "Behold, he goeth before you" (Matt. 28:7). When we live by the sacrament of every second, the risen Christ will teach us when to move forward, when to proceed. But blessed are we when we have let him teach us this greater lesson—*never precede his inner lead.*

The Prayer That Is Always Answered

When we have told him that we want never to get ahead of his footsteps, never to have a vacation from his plans, always to make each second a point of sacred service—when we have told him this in all sincerity—he will bring us to the center of holy simplification that is perfect concord with his perfect will.

Nowhere else but in this center are we truly remade, our hearts really quieted, and heaven's pure harmony so gloriously restored. Here the urgent sirens of the world's emergencies, the babble of hucksters, the calliope of entertainment, the "hup, two, three, four" of many sergeants fades away. There is a whisper here. It is life's Holy Orderer guiding our going. This is the still small voice of the Lord directing our lives to the unhurried serenity, which is Christ himself doing his work through us. Now we will not panic. All we have to do is to remake the world. But Christ is at work on this work. He goes before us. We follow his lead.

Heaven has not left us to wonder how we enter this sacred place. This gate swings wide at the prayer for perfect integration.

This is the prayer that God always answers. He cannot fail to respond because he made us for this prayer. This prayer is the key to the divine workshop. It is the prayer by which each day and every second is placed at the disposal of all eternity.

This petition by which our lives are made truly effective for Christ's sake is the simple prayer of the one-willed life. It is our single calling. It asks our all, but it is worth all. Our lives have reached their true efficiency when we have learned to pray, and mean it:

> Lord Jesus come into my heart.
> Right now, and forever,
> Have your way in my soul. Amen.